Susie Uses Manners

Written and Illustrated by Jb Shane

This is Susie. Susie always uses her manners.

Susie uses manners at home.

Susie uses manners at school.
May I use the restroom?

Susie uses manners at the library.
Shhh....

Susie uses manners when talking to her mom.

Susie uses manners when talking to her dad.

Susie uses manners out in public.
That is a beautiful dress.
Thank you!

Susie uses manners when playing with others.

Susie uses manners when she burps.
Burp
Excuse me!
cola

Susie uses manners when someone gets hurt.
I'm sorry! I didn't mean to. Are you ok?

Susie uses manners when asking for something.

Susie uses manners when she needs help from others.

Now let's play along with Susie and practice how to use manners in different situations.

What should Susie say when someone gives her a gift?

That's right! Susie should say thank you when someone gives her a gift!

Thank you!

What should Susie say if she accidentally breaks something?

That's right! Susie should say sorry when she breaks something.

What should Susie say if she wants some more juice?

That's right! Susie should say please if she wants more of something.
Please may I have more juice?.

See? Using manners is super easy!

Susie uses manners because it's the respectful thing to do.

When we use manners it makes other people feel good, and it makes us feel good too!

So be like Susie and make sure you use your manners too!